꧁꧂

THE SHIP
AND THE
SAFE
HARBOR

꧁꧂

THE SHIP
AND THE
SAFE
HARBOR

A Celebration of Toni Morrison
in Interviews and Reviews from
*Belles Lettres: A Review of Books
by Women* (1988–1995)

*Angels Carabi, Jewelle Gomez
and Faye Moskowitz, contributors
Edited by Janet Palmer Mullaney*

On the Cover: Photo of Toni Morrison by Brian Lankei from the dust jacket of *Jazz*.

CONTENTS

FOREWORD

*"It is that quality of being both the ship
and the safe harbor that I like in
my imaginary women."*
—Toni Morrison, in discussing Jazz

Toni Morrison's vibrancy and vision, expansive soul, and keen sense of humor pervade this engrossing series of conversations on her works with Professor Emerita Angels Carabi of the University of Barcelona. *Belles Lettres* was also blessed that two more creative powerhouses — contributing editors Jewelle Gomez and Faye Moskowitz — wrote perceptive reviews of two groundbreaking novels by the greatly missed Nobel laureate (*Beloved* and *Jazz*). Morrison's wisdom envelops us and — alas — remains timely. Consider this exchange from the 1988 interview:

Death is an ever-present element in your works. Is this awareness rooted particularly in African culture? We adjust ourselves to the fact that it is there all the time. The likelihood of dying, for black people, is not whimsical. It was already very excessive in slavery times. I have two sons, and the probability of either one of them living until they are forty—and I mean being killed—is one out of thirty. It's very real. The Klan is still out there. That all sounds like "oh sensational, sensational," but the fact is that every Black woman knows that if she has a son, there are possibilities that he will not make it. Not to speak of natural death by natural causes—bad housing, illness, and all that."

Or these observations from her 1994 interview on *Beloved*:

"I was traveling around the United States after *Beloved* came out. Everywhere I would go, there was a picture of a confederate soldier on a horse in the middle of the town. Everybody has a monument to every little thing. There is a huge wall to all the veterans, but there is not one bench where we can sit down and think about those people. There is now some effort to do that, but it's like you don't have to pay respect to your ancestors.

They are just waiting there for you to ask them to do something,
but if you don't know them, don't honor them, don't think of
them, mourn them, or praise them, then you are like a cripple.
A public monument or a private monument is needed, not just
to the ancestors we know, but to all those we don't. That's a big
gap, a disjunction in the history."

Yes, society must change radically before this appalling reality
crumbles. And while making that happen, we can rejoice in
Morrison's unparalleled legacy, which lights our way. In her
Stockholm lecture, the newly minted laureate wrote "We die.
That may be the meaning of life. But we do language."
Did she ever!! —Janet Palmer Mullaney, founding editor of
Belles Lettres: A Review of Books by Women

CHAPTER 1
The Bluest Eye, Sula, Song of Solomon, Tar Baby
Interview with Angels Carabi (1986)

*I*n your novels, especially Song of Solomon *and* Tar Baby, *there is a sense of being comfortable with the world of magic, with the supernatural. Was this part of growing up?*
In my recollection, a vivid distinction was made between the actual world and the possible world, by which one certainly felt enchanted. Reality was much enhanced by a perception that included an intimacy with the possible world. These things were discredited in school because they were not seen as religion. What was important was that you could talk about dreams in a revelatory way, to gather information for yourself, your family, your neighbors. I don't mean with a Freudian interpretation; in dreams the information is right there. When I began to write, particularly the third book [*Song of Solomon*], I got strong enough to incorporate this quality in my writing. I wanted to represent that African feeling. It was not possible to talk about a certain time, a historical time, without including that perception. Well-educated Black people will not accept that because it reminds them of their ignorant, barefooted slave past, but their grandmother's life was like that. [*Morrison laughs.*]
Magic also served the function of narrative strategy; for me, it could give my book something that I always wished, which is a sense of adventure within the Black culture that functions in an imaginative way. In the first book [*The Bluest Eye*] there is no magic; it only exists for the children and it is not to be taken seriously. It is their last resort and is very personal. In *Sula,* I use it for natural causes (nature goes awry), but I did it much more deliberately in *Song of Solomon.* In *Tar Baby,* the world of magic is left for the native people: Therese, Son.

In The Bluest Eye, *the reader can hear the music of the family, the music of the community gossiping, the music of Claudia's mother (even, or especially, when she fusses). In comparison to* The Bluest Eye, Sula *is a silent book. Maybe this is why Nel's cry at the*

"

end sounds so loud — and releases the tension that has held the book together.

Some of what you say is enlightening to me, especially about *Sula* being a silent book, because I think it is. I know this was very much in my mind, since in my writing I'm trying to recollect the ambience of life, using bits and pieces of my own experience. The presence of music is very important for me. As a matter of fact, my mother was always singing different tunes to me. Those were the days that you could walk in the street and hear people singing on their porches, or as they walked. When the mailman in my neighborhood walked by, I ran and looked through the window and heard him, singing "profundo." People have stopped singing because there are records. Singing was taken for granted when I was a kid, so I wanted this to be part of my books.

I didn't think about it in *Sula* because there is another kind of intense love and terror in the relationship between Nel and Sula. I had no literary precedent for friendship between women, and my idea was to try to show how valuable it was. I thought I would make a book about two women not at all alike but who loved one another. At one point, they cannot talk to each other, but I wanted readers to miss Sula so they can share Nel's despair. I could have made nice, loving girls, but it seemed to me much more theatrical to make them different to the point that their friendship was harmed. For once what a woman said to another was not about men, like how to get one, but about themselves, Your interpretation of *Sula* being a silent book is accurate, because there is this effort to contain something that is new because it is too big, and I had tried to move away from the ordinary.

In Song, *the music transcends the limits of the community and brings echoes of the past. Milkman discovers his family origins through the song the children sing in the streets of Shalimar.*

Yes, *Song* was about that. It was about the song and history, about genealogy. I made a song that adjusted to the plot of the story.

The music acts as a link to the community. Can you compare the function of the written language to that of the music?

I think the reason for the existence of written art is because of the loss of music. Music was information. It was almost never entertainment. It was articulation, and so much of the music that was powerful had no words. It is not a contradiction. Everybody knew the meaning of the sound. It is the earliest moan, everybody's cry. When there is pain, there are no words; all pain is the same. Everybody expresses pain at a certain level, but to qualify the kind of pain that is ours, and to shape it so it has an effect, is what is genuine. For Black people, it is what we call "moaning." Its tone, its African language, is what needs to be reflected. In *Song*, music takes the shape of a family tree.

But my feeling is that music at one time was private. It was played on these records that nobody bought but us, and —most important — music was the one art form that we determined. The musicians told other musicians when to get off the stage. They made the decisions and established the criteria, which is why there are no real mediocre [Black] musicians; you could not even get into that arena because the standards were so high.

This is not true of literature, because it is always filtered through white sensibilities: the publisher is white and is not going to buy anything that he doesn't think will sell. He needs traditional readership. Even if it is something exotic, it has to be something that white people are interested in. Even slave narratives were not read by Black people; they were addressed to a white audience. It was persuasive, important, but you didn't feel it. Music was always an interior, individual thing. Improvisation is certainly the most individual thing you can think of. Even the person who is doing it doesn't know what is coming next; but at the same time it has to work with the construct of the ensemble, or of the audience, because the audience was very much part of it. Music had annihilated the normal individual collective tension by permitting the listener the entrance, the access to it. Part of it was the active participation of the audience singing or swinging or saying "yeah" or whatever. When it became beloved by white people, white musicians began to play it and it became white property: American music. The change it underwent was interesting and fascinating too, but there was a loss also. There was a need among Blacks to be comfortable with one another without using the oppressor's language. It seems to me that the [Black] novel plays that part because music is still alive but is not exclusively ours. So, it must be possible to write a book published by a white publisher and edited by a white editor (whom I respect) but a book that is "for" Black people, in the sense that I use my criteria as if I were a musician.

When you write, do you have in mind that some of your readers are going to be white?
No, I don't. I never had this problem, but I have it now. Before, it was natural. I was determined to write and I worked all right for the first three books. By the time I did the fourth [*Tar Baby*], I had gotten a lot of attention. People knew me, had written about my work. I felt an unsolicited entrance, and I had to deliberately exorcise them.

Can you explain the presence of your white characters in Tar Baby*?*
I had to have those white characters because they were part of the original "Tar Baby" story. I wasn't looking to include white characters as a flow. (It would have been kind of funny; if they don't put me in their books, why should I include them?) I was quite content to continue to write books that way, but when I got really obsessed with that story — believe me it was this incredible story, a prophecy — I put my mind in it and I just said: "Well, I have to do it and do it the best way I can." Nevertheless, the perception would be from inside out.

Something that is also present in your works is silence. Often silence emerges at moments of tremendous pain for the characters (Cholly being rejected by his father, Hagar rejected by Milkman).
Part of that very full, very rich silence is the absence of speech, which says more than words. I always want moments of partnership between myself and the readers. I want to yank them and shut the door; but once they are in, they have to provide emotional information and vision. Sometimes I force the reader to see by just giving a few clues, the way you hear a told story. Not everything is in it. In told stories you share the creativity. "How

loud was the thunder?" you question yourself. I wanted very much to have this oral origin to be in the text. In some places you can do it with the language by using certain words, but in others I encourage an emotion that I assume the reader will be able to capture because he or she has probably had a similar experience. It's like when I describe a sexual scene. I have to assume that a reader's sexuality is much more sensual than mine — because it is theirs, it is the one that matters. So I don't want to take it away but to bring it in. And then it has the quality of a heightened sensuality, not because I describe it so, but because I have not described it. So silence is also imaginative space.

On the other hand, the way your characters sound, often in dialogue, is powerful. The reader can hear them talk.
It has to do with the language. The American English Black people speak has been ridiculed as a sign of stupidity, you know, like lower class, but to me it seems very powerful. It struck my mind even as a child. Standard English is sterile. I don't mean that English is a sterile language, but the everyday speech of people is. I lived in a mixed neighborhood and I was always amazed at the language that people spoke, regardless of their education. The metaphors were fabulous: They used pictures that would make your mind jump. So it occurred to me that I would use the language and strip it to its gleaming power. This was not a question of subject–verb agreement. It's not really pronunciation either: it is rhythm, and an emphasis. That's where the difference in the language is, and it also has a sound. If I use adverbs all the time it sort of waters the prose down. But if you put the cruelty in the sentence — the humor, the menace, or the ambivalence — then you don't need other things. The language of Black people is extraordinary, a truly theatrical language.

Nature, it seems to me, becomes a metaphor in your works for indicating that everything is interrelated. The failure of the marigolds to grow echoes the death of Pecola's baby. Sula's arrival is announced by a plague of robins. Milkman achieves oneness with nature as a sign of his maturity. Son is symbolically being born in the arms of the water lady. Can you talk about your perception of nature?

I am not sure how I developed my passion for explaining nature. Some say it is a backdrop and not terribly original. Milkman, for instance, goes first into the cave. Then he walks up, then he goes into water, and finally he leaps into the air. My need to write about nature became progressively insistent, to the point that I felt nature was conveying a reclamation of the world. The world reclaims everything, and part of it is the place where we live, right here. In *Song,* Milkman discovers America when he grasps the meaning of the names of the towns he sees in the south, which goes beyond the geographic and inanimate world. By and by, I got finished with that type of interpretation. I didn't want to fake it. One can have literary illusions, and I knew the risk of creating history in a deliberate way. In *Tar Baby,* I needed a special place, a background that had the ancient qualities to confront the modern perspective of the story and its characters.

Sometimes nature misleads the characters.

Well, the characters can misread it. Part of their ability to read it depends on their perception of themselves. The more perceptive human beings are about themselves, the cleverer they are at seeing. Milkman could never have saved his life if he had not been listening to his surroundings. To be able to fly, he had to build up his skills as he went on, in a natural sense. The assumption being that he learns enough about himself.

The reader senses your need to free your characters from the Judeo-Christian tradition. This seems to be effectively conveyed by their having biblical names, ironically, inappropriate to their nature.

Black people were very inventive and almost "ad hoc" about religion. They took from Christianity things that they could use and concentrated on what meant something for them. The Virgin, they could not get into; virginity was not something that they valued. But the Mother of God, that they took seriously. They were extremely loyal to the Bible for a number of reasons, not only religious. It was against the law to teach Blacks to read, and you could die if you learned. So access to books, except for the Bible, was forbidden. Whites thought, I am convinced, that you had to write everything down because you were defective and couldn't remember.

This freedom from the written expression was also true for the musicians. They could read music, but they would not look at what was written because when you write it, it freezes, and it will never be better than that. Once Miles Davis said that he didn't own any of his records, because a record was just the way that he played it then, and he would not play it that way again. There is this insistence on invention and recreation. All this to say that memory and change were more important this sort of record, then. The Bible offered a fatalistic view of life. Christian religion is a double-edged sword. The Church provided things for Black people and it also became an educational thing. On the other hand, Christianity as a practice was way over their heads. Somebody was complaining about the absence of religion in my books—not that I never mentioned it, but that I never give it a dominant place. I am not sure how I would feel about it.

Your characters move away from their biblical names. Is this done on purpose?
[She laughs.] I guess I do it subliminally. I just know my characters' names, I don't pick them. They come to me in some spooky ways. I knew Sula's name instantly. I later learned something interesting. In describing Sula's character to an African historian, I told her that I was creating a woman who was perceived in a different way. It was very difficult because I didn't want her to be a conventional villainess, some kind of greedy person that wants more. I wanted her to have a quality like water, so that she took the shape of whatever held her; if it was a cup, she would have a cup shape. If a spoon, she would have a spoon shape. The historian asked me, "What do you call her?" I said, "Sula." "Well that's interesting, she said. "Do you know that there is an African language in which the word for water is 'sula' "? And then she said, "Have you heard that song *Sulame, Sulame?*" "Yes," I said. "Well, it means water run." But I didn't know it. So I always trusted those immediate names, which are very imaginatively

chosen. Usually I know them, but if I don't, I just have to wait until they tell me their names. Ultimately, and this is part of the choice, they have this other quality of ironic play, because they are not predictable. Biblical names are based on what they are called. The only trustworthy names are nicknames, because they have been chosen. They come out of something that has happened. They are real names because it might take a long time before you get one. These names are based on some incident, physical characteristic, or tendency.

The grotesqueness of your educated, light-skinned characters (Geraldine, First Corinthians, Helen Wright) has provoked controversy. There are those who think that you try to present education as a destructive force.
[Morrison laughs.]
These characters are terrible. Well, nobody knew about our own history. White education had displaced it. I think that the light education issue began when one had to go to school. There were choices to go to special schools. White society always chose light-skinned people, especially women, because they were less of a threat than men. There's a whole line of books in this country about discrediting Black people for their Black skin, and about the tragic mulatta, light-skinned women who had a very complicated life. The Black woman never appeared, because they thought there was something impure about her. I was interested in restoring some currency, some value to a whole number of people. Geraldine is close to Helen Wright. They were very determined women who tried to get away from the darker-skinned people who were shown contempt. This means despising people like Pecola.

Your characters go beyond the norm.
I'm not interested in the norm, but more important than that, I find these people extremely powerful. Some call them bigger than life, but it doesn't seem that they are as big as life. Life is very big. These so-called "normal" people put out those that they don't want to be bothered about. They want to read about Geraldines. But I can tell you that in my youth I met more interesting people than I know now. They were more passionate, they loved more. I

never knew people that were alike. I remember women talking about other women and the stories were really wild — all of them were like Anna Magnani's film roles. It was incredible. Some of them were quiet, some of them were mad, some are still mad. It's crazy being a woman in this society. If you are a Black *and a* woman... [*she laughs*].

The reader accepts your eccentrics.
The characters are under pressure. You get a definition of yourself, you think you're "A," but something happens, and somebody calls this into question. You think you are afraid. What is loyalty? What is betrayal? What is unlicensed about love? Finally, you decide that your child would be better dead than alive, as Eva, in *The Bluest Eye*, does. Well, people do that all the time. They don't kill their sons but they say, "If you don't do it my way you go out." I just make it thick and theatrical, and then the reader is off the hook. He or she thinks "Well ha! That's terrible! Oh! *I* wouldn't do that!" But maybe there is a kind of mirror that makes people focus on the nature of the relationship.

I had a student who said she had been sexually abused and couldn't talk about it. I told her not to try to bear that kind of thing alone. She said she had been attracted to my class because of my books. She was a white girl. White girls didn't talk. It is certainly not true now, but this had to do with what we were talking about before, which is silence as a virtue. Women have always struggled with the lesson to be silent and [wanting] to talk at the same time. The penalties for talking were incredible. The traditional woman is quiet. She fusses with her husband, with her child; but the virtue of the silent mother is universal. I have this problem with female students all the time. They are sabotaging themselves. They really don't believe they can speak for themselves or make judgments, because women are not trained for it.

It's not our world or our language, and the more scholarly we become, we translate it into masculinity. "She's very objective ... very *[Morrison laughs]* ... all these words that mean she thinks like a man, acts like a man, and so on. So it's very difficult to give ourselves permission to talk.

Can you talk about the myth of the blind horsemen that you use in
Tar Baby*? I couldn't find any references regarding its sources.*
Mythology is like music. In it there is something important. In *Tar
Baby*, I made the myth of blind men based on a newspaper story I
read. A ship that was carrying a circus in the Caribbean, sank, and
nobody got out except the horses. I said to myself, suppose not
only the horses swam ashore, but that men had survived too. What
would they have become?

*But aren't myths supposed to come out of a collective
consciousness? How do you feel about the responsibility of
making up one?*
[Laughs heartily.] Oh!, I don't think I will do that again. It's true
that myth has to come out of collectivity, but I couldn't wait.
[Continues laughing.] I had to get one then!

*Both Milkman and Son achieve a mythical quality, which none of
your "young heroines" achieves (only Pilot and Therese, but they
play an ancestor-like role.) Are you implying that your young
heroes are more suited to carry on the myth than your young
heroines?*
Sula could be a mythical figure, but she is too young. Young
women are difficult to me in that line: it's difficult for anybody.
The twenties are difficult. It is a wonderful time in life, but nothing
is going on. No shape, no direction. So I have the worst time to get
that woman's substance. I can show her, but I don't want to do it
flat. I wanted somebody that could attract you and that could
annoy you.

Are you talking about Jadene in Tar Baby*?*
Yes. You can't feel passion for someone that does not feel passion,
so I had to create it in her. It took forever. The trouble I had with
her suggests this discrepancy of mine, because I have to create
basing my ideas on the people that I know, and on myself. When I
was twenty, I knew what I did, but I didn't have a vision of self.
Then I got married, I got divorced, and I had my own self. At that
time, in my twenties, I was doing wonderful things, and it was a
wonderful period, but it was like there was nobody inside.

[Laughs] That's my perception of it. You know, you have to have
some connection in order to write.

*Death is an ever-present element in your works. Is this awareness
rooted particularly in African culture?*
In this place, we adjust ourselves to the fact that it is there all the
time. The likelihood of dying, for Black people, is not whimsical.
It was already very excessive in slavery times. I have two sons, and
the probability of either one of them living until they are forty—and
I mean being killed—is one out of thirty. It's very real. The Klan is
still out there. That all sounds like "oh sensational, sensational,"
but the fact is that every Black woman knows that if she has a son,
there are possibilities that he will not make it. Not to speak of
natural death by natural causes—bad housing, illness, and all that.

*What did the sixties mean for the Black woman? What changes
did they bring to her status and her perception of herself?*
I guess it was visibility. What one did was done not only self-
consciously, but with an exterior consciousness, so that people
were aware of their actions at last.

How do you view the eighties?
There's a much more mature attitude. The movement now is not
the idea of women's sisterhood together, but that the capitalist
industry promotes hierarchies. To play into that you have to be
extremely competitive.

*Mobility in space becomes a common factor in the works of the
eighties. Alice Walker's* The Color Purple *takes place in the South
and in Africa; Paule Marshall's* Praisesong for the Widow *sets the
action from White Plains to Granada; Ntozake Shange's*
Sassafrass, Cypress and Indigo *moves from San Francisco to New
York;* Tar Baby *takes place in the South, in New York, and in the
Caribbean. Can you comment on that?*
I'm so glad! Otherwise, all of us would be claustrophobic. Sula is
in this one room. That seemed to be natural because women
stayed at home, but now they are moving out. It is that quality of

being both the ship and the safe harbor that I like in my imaginary women.

ANGELS CARABI is a professor emerita of English literature at the University of Barcelona. Her special interest is women writers of color from the U.S., many of whom she has interviewed. This interview was taped at the Alternative Museum of New York City in August of 1986. It appeared in *Belles Lettres: A Review of Books by Women,* 08-31-1988; Vol. 3; No. 6, pp. 8-9.

CHAPTER 2 — *Beloved*

1986 Interview with Angels Carabi

In Beloved *you move back into history and plunge into the period of slavery. It seems that by writing about that period, you bring up a collective pain that had been silenced within the Black community but that was always there, kept as an unspoken burden: almost as a ghostlike presence.*

Yes, I thought that in the folklore and in the songs and in early poetry or lyrics, there was never much mention of the "middle passage." The poems I know about this period are recent — after the 1960s. So there was a part of history, of that journey from Africa to America, that Black people themselves had never spoken about.

I understand that omission, because to dwell on it would perhaps paralyze you to the point of not being able to survive everyday life. It was too painful to remember, yet I had the impression that it was something that needed to be thought about by Afro-Americans. With *Beloved,* I am trying to insert this memory that was unbearable and unspeakable into the literature. Not only to write about a woman who did what Sethe did, but to have the ghost of the daughter return as a remnant of a period that was unspoken. It was a silence within the race. So it's a kind of healing experience. There are certain things that are repressed because they are unthinkable, and the only way to come free of that is to go back and deal with them.

Memory has a dual function. On the one hand, to remember painful periods generates suffering.... Yet remembering has a healing quality; suffering provides information and ultimately offers self-knowledge.

Oh yes, absolutely. And then that makes it possible to live completely. Part of you is dead if you don't remember. Part of your mind is vacant, so it is not complete. So the pain is worth it, because the healing is great.

Beloved's arrival stimulates Sethe's memory.

Some of it. Paul D is there before, and at least Sethe begins to think about certain things, like the plantation. Beloved comes after Paul D, and she is like a catalyst. She opens up everybody's vulnerability.

I see Beloved as an individual character, also as a ghost — but also as a representative of all the women that went through the middle passage whose stories have remained silent.
It could be. I wanted a baby in human body, without past or future (having been killed so young), and also to be the embodiment of the past. It is indeed what she says: a new segment of the history that has been unlived and unattended to. And because it is so fresh, much more painful to handle.

Can the fact that she has this demonic quality be associated with the painful aspect of remembering?
Oh yes, not only with that but with her death itself. She was violently "disremembered." It's like the history of the Middle Passage. All those people who threw themselves into the sea had been violently ignored; no one praised them, nobody knows their names, nobody can remember them, not in the United States or in Africa. Millions of people disappeared without a trace, and there is not one monument anywhere to pay homage to them, because they never arrived safely on shore. So it's like a whole nation that is under the sea. A nameless, violent extermination.

Can Beloved's redeeming quality be associated with the fact that she provokes understanding of history among the people around her?
Oh, yes. She makes them face up to the things they have been avoiding. They have to, in a sense, grow up in her presence. Her physical presence is so persistent that she cannot be ignored anymore, so they have to deal with her.

On the ship there is no air, no water, and no space in which to move. This brings echoes of death, of a living death. Were you trying to establish a close association between death and the ship?

Between the ship and the grave. When Beloved talks to Sethe or Denver, they think she has come back from the grave. And they ask what it was like over there. Her language fits into their conception of life after death. And since it was a dying place, I wanted the association between the physical journey on the slave ships and the grave to be very strong.

Can you talk about the water imagery in the novel? Sethe breaks water when she gives birth to Denver, and her bladder "fills to capacity" when she meets Beloved.
Obviously I wanted Sethe to be re-experiencing birth. The other part has to do with the African conviction regarding reincarnation. It is believed that, in particular, children or young people who die uneasily return out of the water in forms of members of your family. Water is a dangerous and haunted place because spirits dwell in it.

Sethe is also a woman who was abandoned by her mother; she remembers her only as a woman in the field.
Yes, and that makes her fierce with her children. The fact that she was abandoned, or that she feels abandoned (she doesn't know her mother) destroys a normal parent–child relation. Her horror is that, maybe, her mother was trying to escape without her. When Sethe has children, she is excessively ferocious about keeping them with her as a kind of reaction to her own feelings of abandonment. So it makes her infanticide much more powerful, because she thinks that by killing her children and herself, she can go to an eternal place where they can be together again without pain. Death would not be termination, merely a change into something else.

When Sethe was living on the plantation she did not have other women to talk with to tell her how to take care of her children. Her impulse to kill Beloved comes out of a woman who is used to making decisions on her own. Would it have been different if Sethe had a community?
Oh yes, she is isolated. When Sethe commits the act, the community rejects her. She is uncivilized in the woman sense of

the word. She doesn't know how to negotiate certain levels of pain,
because she has never been advised. If Baby Suggs had been there,
she would have understood Sethe's heart breaking every time she
had to tie her children to the well so she could work and watch
them, to make sure they weren't hurt. Sethe has less than a month
of neighborhood life: that's all she ever knew of a community of
her peers. Her independence is such that when she leaves the
house after the act, the women recognize that solitary excessive
pride and reject her. It's only when Sethe feels so beaten down and
that excess has gone the other way that they come and rescue her.

*Sethe is the only child conceived in love. She was named after her
father. Her name is one of her own, conceived out of a loving
relationship. Can you talk about the relevance of having a name of
your own, given with love and tenderness? Slaves did not have
names of their own.*

If slaves came with their own names they were ignored. People just
named them something they wanted to. The purpose was to keep
families separated in order to control them, and to give the slaves
the last name of the master, as property. If I give you another
name, then I own you; this is why Black people had nicknames,
names that they gave themselves. Stamp Paid is a classic example.
He's born Joshua, and he does something that is memorable: he
changes his own name to Stamp Paid. Paul D's name, for instance
— all these letters — is a sign of contempt. So it's rare and delicious
to have a name that is given to you by a parent, based on a love
relationship or maybe given by somebody in your family. Then
you earn your name; it's not just a name of a white person attached
to you. Baby Suggs is another example. Her name is Janey
Whirlow, but Janey she does not recognize and Whirlow was the
name of whoever owned her. She was married to a man named
Suggs, and he used to call her Baby Suggs. So that's her name. It's
her resistance.

*When Sethe tells her story to Denver and Beloved she recovers
her Mama's language, which she thought she had forgotten. Can
you talk about the relevance of recovering the original language?*

It is a suggestion that all these languages, including cultures that had been wiped out, can be recovered only through an active effort of the will. Sethe is, in fact, telling a story, and by narrating it she sort of talks herself into being. She doesn't talk about the past ever; she just warns Denver, but her daughter does not want to hear either. When Paul D comes, she begins to think a little bit about the past. When Beloved appears, she has to tell them more, a little more each time, and suddenly certain things from her childhood just come back. Even though she can't really remember the language, she remembers what it said. She remembers what she understood and that becomes a reclamation of a past. I don't know how many people, except maybe Sixo, could remember the language. I don't know how many Afro-Americans could speak these other languages. That disruption of history is very, very painful, but we can reclaim ourselves by narrative, by active effort, by telling.

Something that is very interesting is that, even though Sethe does not remember the language, the African past is unconsciously being retained through the image of the dancing antelope that she relives before giving birth to Denver. This image is associated with Sethe's mother's dance. So part of the African past is transmitted through images.
Through images and with the help of Beloved's presence. If Beloved had not shown up, Sethe could never have remembered this. But the past comes back. So Sethe can gather bits and pieces of a life when she was a little girl. I think she's lucky because she is made to remember by herself. It would be interesting if she could pass this on to Denver. But I have the feeling that Denver goes out to college and forgets about it all (*laughter*).

Africa is seen as a place where women gathered flowers in freedom and played in the long grass before the white men arrived. It is freedom that brings the idea of Africa as a lost paradise.
Yes, that's right. Whatever the difficulties were, they were *their* difficulties and not somebody else's. No one could possibly tell what the place would have been like if the white men had never

arrived there. You don't know it because it was beaten up so early. If they had been left alone, maybe they would have stayed agricultural. It may be a little too romantic to think about Africa as a kind of Eden, before corruption, the cradle of humanity. And sure enough, it was a place with confrontations, but it was not a conquered place where other people's imaginations worked on it instead of their own. Nevertheless, what Sethe remembers before she was captured is a picture of a community.

She experiences the loss of her husband as well as of her sons, yet the losses seem less than those of her mother and daughter. Does this mean that the bonds between mother and daughter are stronger?

Well, she doesn't know whether Halley is living or dead. The loss of her sons is painful, but they are boys, who always leave anyway. But she hit the boys with the shovel and cut the baby girl's throat. I could have made the baby a boy. So I am not sure that I intended to say anything about the bond between mother and son or mother and daughter.

Sethe's sense of guilt turns her into Beloved's victim, and their roles reverse. Does Sethe feel that she deserves to be forgiven by Beloved? Can she be?

No, not by Beloved! (*laughter*). No, she is insatiable. Sethe could never give her enough. She represents 350 years of indifference, so it would take 350 years to fill her up. Sethe gives her life to Beloved to the exclusion of Denver. It's herself she cannot forgive. She tried very hard to say, "this is the right thing to do." And she was not repentant at all, but in the face of that child — not the neighbors, not Paul D — she would have had to explain and explain, and she could never explain enough. Now she is not so sure of her deed. With Beloved's presence she feels happy and is able to tell herself: "See, she came back, and I don't have to explain a thing." She is the one left to forgive herself. Her lover can't give her that.

I don't find this sense of guilt in Eva (in your novel Sula*) when she burns her son alive. What's the difference?*

He is not a baby. He is grown and he is going to be a burden to himself and to her. And Eva is very arrogant; she names everybody (*laughter*).

At the end, when Sethe tries to kill Mr. Bodwin, it seem to me that she exorcises the past by addressing her anger against him instead of against her children as she did in the past. Does this reflect a change of attitude in Black people: instead of self-mutilation, addressing the anger at the source of their misery?

Maybe, but she can't kill her daughter a second time (*laughter*). She just directs her fury at the person whom she thinks is going to destroy her. She is in love with her daughter now; if she loves her daughter, the woman Beloved, she loves herself. Then she can turn her head and direct her anger at the sources she thinks are the cause of her misery, rather than escaping it by doing something violent.

Sethe must confront her past to achieve self-knowledge, to save herself. When this past is assumed, Beloved can disappear. Would you agree with this?

Beloved has no place there now. Sethe is now going to concentrate on taking care of herself, the beloved that is inside her, which is her. She is the beloved, not the child. The past is returned and buried again, or gone.

Is the past gone or assumed ... incorporated?

The book, at the end, assumes it is gone. Sethe doesn't, maybe. The last part of it suggests that they will not get rid of the whole thing. It's there, somewhere. The least gesture, the least look. I don't know. Maybe Sethe will be able to put both things together — admit what she did and go on from there. Maybe I'm more optimistic about her than about the whole race. I was traveling around the United States after *Beloved* came out. Everywhere I would go, there was a picture of a confederate soldier on a horse in the middle of the town. Everybody has a monument to every little thing. There is a huge wall to all the veterans, but there is not one bench where we can sit down and think about those people. There is now some effort to do that, but it's like you don't have to pay respect to your ancestors. They are just waiting there for you to ask them to do something, but if you don't know them, don't honor them, don't think of them, mourn them, or praise them, then you are like a cripple. A public or a private monument is needed, not just to the ancestors we know, but to all those we don't. That's a big gap, a disjunction in the history.

Is this then a story to pass on? But if it is, wouldn't the burden of the past make us unable to live the present?
It's both. If you just dwell on the past, you can't go forward. If you confront the past, there is a possibility to move on. So I said that this is not a story to pass on, but it's like a warning to Black people. This is not a story to pass on, to give to the next one, yet the irony is that it is not a story to pass by. So it has both meanings.

Can you talk about the role of the community in Beloved? *In fact, the community increases Sethe's isolation.*
The community makes judgments. It's like a chorus. The survival of individuals is dependent on the community. Sethe make a valiant effort to live without it. And she can't. They reject her, too, because she's behaving in a very proud way. She is saying to the community: "I'll get along without you," and they know it, so they let her try. And then, when she is beaten down enough, they don't kick her out; by and large they support her. Baby Suggs was a very big part of the community. When she dies, Sethe is all alone, leading the solitary life of widow. This is hubris, so the community lets her know that they think she is too proud.

When Denver finally leaves the house, the community recognizes that Sethe can't do everything by herself, and then they know that there is no pride. Sethe learns the lesson and makes it possible for the community to come. They exorcise what they consider the demon of the past, which has hurt her beyond endurance. Maybe they have a sort of thermometer to measure how much misery a person can take (*laughter*).

Are you implying then that the community does not reject her for her deed, but because of her pride?

The community does not reject her because of the killing of the child but because of how she responded to that murder. She did not come home and weep and say: "Oh my God, look at what I did!" She didn't say: "Help me!.... I don't know why I did that." She just walked out of the house with her head up, went to jail, got taken out, came home, got a job, and went on living like that. And even when she comes out of the house, they are watching her. They sing but they don't have any words. They recognize the beginning of arrogance, and that keeps them away from her.

Let's move on to Paul D. In a way, he redeems Sethe from a haunted past, leading her into the present. At the same time he's helping himself because he's been wandering for so long.
Yes, he's been going from place to place, and when he finds Sethe he can help her; he can inhabit her body, fill it. Which is what you don't do when you are very busy.

Fear of loss generates a hunger for love. Beloved is so hungry for love that she destroys Sethe. Are you implying that if you become possessive about the person you love, you end up destroying him or her?
One of the most profound devastations of oppression is how love is distorted. If you love something too much you'll kill it. Or if you love it too little, because you are afraid, you can lose it. You don't enjoy; you do it slyly. Like when Paul D is in prison: he can't even love nature, just a little bit of the moon because if he loves it too much he will lose it, and you need a bit left over for the next step. So you become emotionally and aesthetically stingy for fear that it too, like everything else, will be taken away. Pain affects one's personal life ... in abused children or whole nations that have been tormented. It is difficult to believe, feel, or trust because you can't go through that pain. So you just withhold the emotion.

Freedom meant the possibility to love. Yes. Exactly.

You seldom include the presence of white people in your books. In Beloved *there are Amy and Mr. and Mrs. Garner, who are understanding people within the limitations of a slavery society.*

There are also Schoolteacher and the nephews, who embody an ultimate form of evil.

Slavery meant lots of losses and prohibitions. But you know there were many white people who hated it and thought it was diminishing to them. They felt as if they were less human and that they were called upon to be hateful. And there were others who had a good time, who loved it because they could feel powerful. To continue living and doing what they wanted, they had to make sure that the people they were abusing were not really people. Many people refused to own slaves and looked down on those who did. Sometimes they bought slaves to free them, or even to ensure that no one else could buy them. People do all sorts of things, and some of them are fine and noble. Mr. Bodwin was the apogee of what the abolitionists were like, spending a lot of time, money, and effort to mitigate those circumstances. Whereas somebody like Schoolteacher just had a good time and felt that he was doing God's work.

He is presented as a rational person who studies slaves' behavior scientifically.

Yes. You see, the Age of Enlightenment was at the same time as the age of racism. In the United States, the Constitution is full of wonderful things about freedom and equality, but it was able to accommodate slavery. There is this fundamental contradiction in 18th-century philosophical thought, because the same people who were going on about Christian love and beatitudes and the rights of man were also slave masters who didn't carry their philosophy all the way through. I use the name of Schoolteacher because racism was pursued in a scholarly fashion. It was taught in theology, in anthropology, in biology, in the Darwinian theory of evolution — in everything. They had accommodated something that would mean its own destruction. Therefore, they had to make special provisions for the people they did not want to be associated with: Blacks and women. Somebody like Schoolteacher in 1850 or 1855 would be very much in line with the mainstream thought. The aberration, the eccentric one, would be Mr. Bodwin.

Can you talk about the role of music in Beloved*? Paul D is a singing man, Amy sings a soothing song for Sethe when she is in pain; Sethe sings to her children a song that Beloved recognizes; the women sing.*

It's a summons. Music is a powerful, magical tool. Singing is soothing; it gets you through a difficult period. But it has a greater power than that, which is like poetry: it allows you to articulate what you are feeling. Paul D makes a song about his relationship with Sethe. The women in *Beloved* avoid the house; they stand outside, but when they get serious they burst into song like a religious exorcism. By song you can make things happen. I heard a singer say that during the Civil Rights Movement, when Black people would get ready to go out and demonstrate — to permit themselves to be humiliated — they would have meetings. And you couldn't get them to do anything unless you would start with a song. And then they understood that it was a call, a clarion call. Music gives you the information you want. It raises your courage; it gives you clarity and focus. Then you are able to go forward into a dangerous situation.

Some of your characters make an effort to "beat" the past. Sethe beats the dough in the mornings as a way to beat back the past. Paul D has this tin heart.

It's always threatening to break out. Memories are always threatening, like dreams. Whatever you are not thinking about in the daytime world comes out in your dreams. If you are serious about not wanting to remember, if you try to contain it, hold it back, it takes activity; you have to work at preventing the past from coming through. If you don't work hard, it will come out in distorted ways. You can't let those memories come back until you are strong enough to deal with them.

There are some isolated points in the book that I would like to ask you about: Sethe's tree on her back reminded me of a family tree, like the words the woman warrior has carved on her back in Maxine Hong Kingston's The Women Warrior. *She carries the family history on her back.*

Well, I used to look at those pictures of people with scars. Sethe is not able to see her tree on her back. She does not feel anything, but she is marked by the history of slavery, written with scars.

Beloved watches two turtles copulate. It is a love act?
(*Laughter*) I don't know. I wanted her to look outside herself for a moment, to see something that was not hers. The reason I chose turtles was because of the contradiction between these big shells that are impenetrable and rough and unromantic, and the two heads so vulnerable and tender. The female head pops out and pats the male's head as he mounts her. Beloved's seduction of Paul D is to get him out, to get rid of anybody that Sethe might be interested in. That scene takes place before the seduction, before she tells Paul D "call me my name." She moves him out of the house; so I wanted to introduce sexuality and sensuality in her mind. And, of course, there is a hint that she's been reared by somebody who used her sexually.

A prevailing sense in the book is of loss.
And possibilities. Loss is the overwhelming pain and then, cut through it in small ways, there is the possibility between Sethe and Paul D of regaining life. After going through all the trauma, he comes back. He's horrified because of what Sethe did; but even knowing that, he comes back to the house to look for her. He really does love her. So with a man like that, there is a sense of possibility. Things go on; we did get through it.

Does Beloved *play a cathartic role for the Afro-American people?*
Yes, the book in general is a kind of way in which we can approach these things. I think there should be a lot ... written about all this, about the middle passage. We can't just wipe it out.... And art can do it. Songs, music, paintings, poetry, or novels could concentrate on that period. And it is our job; it is not the white people's job. This one is ours. Black people have to do it.

Don't you think that white people could write about the period of the Middle Passage as well?

Maybe yes, from their point of view. I would love to see a book a by a white person in which the author imagines the situation. A captain on a slave ship, a person that makes it intelligible to me, instead of rationalizing it and defending it. Asking "What was it really like?" I would love to see a contemporary novel by a white woman revealing what it was like to be a slaveowner's wife but to write about it honestly — not in a grandiose or a glamorous way, but in a way that explores the interior of life. In fact there is a book called *Middle Passage*, which I haven't read yet but that I'm very interested in, not because of the historical data ... but because of the interior life.

And how this affects the present, how the past can be clarified. That's right. There will always be a stumbling block, not just racial sub-knowledge, if you try to forget all that. But nobody wants to do it ... to go back and try to remember all that stuff. You think that you might go under, that you might be devastated. When I was writing the book, I thought that some parts were going to be too difficult to deal with. But in those moments I kept saying to myself: "all I have to do is to think about the people who lived there, who lived through it. If they could live it, I could write about it."

[*Belles Lettres* / Vol. 9 No. 3 / 04-30-1994 / p. 38]

BELOVED — The Mysticism and Magic
of African Thought
A review by Jewelle Gomez (1988)

*B*eloved is a ghost story. Its *ha'ants* include the spirits of slavery, race hatred, misogyny, and grief as well as the heroine's daughter, who has died 19 years earlier. Under a cloying blossom of gothic mysticism, Morrison hints at then lays bare the legacy of the runaway slaves of the Sweet Home plantation of Kentucky. As any good ghost story should be, it is compelling and chilling.

Young, pregnant Sethe sends her three children ahead with other escaping slaves to live with their freed grandmother, Baby Suggs, in Ohio. Sethe is caught, raped, and beaten but still escapes, delivering her baby with the help of an itinerant white girl making her own way to freedom. In her escape Sethe leaves behind her husband, Halle, who fails to appear at their appointed meeting place, and two others who are caught and murdered by the callous new owner of Sweet Home. This is enough life for any one lifetime, yet Sethe's new freedom is then threatened by the arrival of her owner, coming to claim his property. Her terror of having her children returned to slavery is borne so deeply within the marrow of who she is that Sethe frantically tries to kill them all, succeeding in the death of only one of her daughters.

In the years that follow, Sethe fills her life with Baby Suggs, her three living children, and the restless ghost of her dead child, who plays pranks like leaving her handprint in cakes and scaring neighbors. Baby Suggs dies, and the two sons, perpetually afraid of their mother and the psychic unrest, abandon the family. Sethe and her daughter, Denver, are left locked in competition and distrust. Paul D., who has also escaped from Sweet Home, finally makes his way to Sethe, and he too is like a ghost, opening up her memory to things she and many around her would rather leave forgotten, including the knowledge that Halle did not escape but remained at Sweet Home and went mad. Paul D. takes his place beside Sethe, reuniting with a happier side of his past. Too full of his own ghosts, he rails against the dead child that dominates the household and drives it out. All is quiet for a time until a young girl appears who calls herself Beloved, the one word on Sethe's daughter's headstone, a word for which Sethe had to barter her own body. She joins the house as a mysterious, alluring woman/child but she soon evolves into a succubus, seeking unqualified devotion and certain destruction:

Rainwater held on to pine needles for dear life and Beloved could not take her eyes off Sethe. Stooping to shake the damper, or snapping sticks for kindlin, Sethe was licked, tasted, eaten by Beloved's eyes. Like a familiar, she hovered, never leaving the room Sethe was in unless required and told to.... In lamplight, and over the flames of the cooking stove, their two shadows clashed and crossed on the ceiling like black swords.

Morrison is undoubtedly one of American literature's premier thinkers and "feelers." Her complex, poetic language makes the feelings of her characters and her own ideas sing. To read her words is to know at once the urgency of Sethe's need to save her children from the death of slavery by killing them. It is also to accept the burden that act must be for Sethe, her shocked neighbors, and her surviving children, who withdraw into their own worlds to disconnect from Sethe's guilt. The ominous presence of Beloved grows like a poisonous flower, alienating Paul D. and almost starving Sethe and Denver, both figuratively and literally.

Morrison dips into the many rivulets of pain that are the overflow of slavery, provoking questions that social historians have yet to tackle strenuously enough to shed much light on the survivors of slavery in America today. And Morrison's success is that she draws not from some remote academic pool of facts but from the simple experience of mother and child, man and woman, friend and neighbor. What does it mean, not to the concept of family but to a mother, to never have had the security of nursing her own child? Or to that child? Sethe remembers her own mother, who was separated from her most of the day, only by the hat she wore working in the fields. Although her mother tried to teach Sethe how to recognize her, she cannot. And there is desperation in Sethe's need to recall her mother, who is now long dead.

What does it do, not to the psyche of a people but to one woman, to never have had the sanctity of her own name? Once freed, Baby Suggs asked her master why he always called her Jenny. He responds simply that it was the name on her tag when he bought her. She has lived separate from that name, somewhere deep inside herself, until freed to take on the surname of the man she called her husband and the name he called her: Baby. This is a simple act, renaming, but one whose importance has been reiterated throughout Black American history, from the Southern tradition of giving children initials instead of first names so they can choose later what they wish to be called, through the Black Power Movement of the '60s, when many Afro-Americans disavowed their slave roots by choosing names from African cultures. Morrison repeatedly points out the cruel and gentle wearing away of life by the denial of names: Paul D.'s name differentiates him from the other slaves on Sweet Home, Paul A. and Paul F. The man who helps escaping Blacks cross the river to freedom adopts the name Stamp Paid. And, of course, Sethe's dead daughter remains nameless, except for her fragmentary epitaph, "Beloved."

Morrison tackles another question, more subtle but equally devastating. When did Africans become Negroes? How African cultures were suppressed and how they survived and blended with European cultures in the United States has been examined somewhat, but the ways of thinking and feeling about these phenomena had to change as well. Morrison skillfully evokes this change by examining the relationship between Sethe and her children and her neighbors.

When we first encounter Stamp Paid, he is an ordinary man but also a heroic figure: the angel of deliverance who has ferried Sethe and Denver to freedom, along with hundreds of others. The community remains so grateful for the lives among them that no door is ever closed to him. That is, until he forgets the horror that lay back on the other side of the river, forgets the death he has helped deliver his people from, and informs Paul D. about Sethe's killing of her child. It is the act of someone removed from the living death of slavery, of someone who has begun to think of himself simply as a citizen. And the rest of the Black community —

which has traditionally welcomed its fleeing sisters and brothers, including Baby Suggs and Sethe — suffers a similar metamorphosis. They lose sight of the simple African joy of sharing and the magic that makes a little go a long way. They become jealous and vain, rejecting Baby Suggs and then Sethe, both of whom remain close enough to their origins to survive with their integrity intact, even if survival means death.

Morrison weaves many delicate aspects of survival, love, and community in a highly poetic manner. The narrative, although told mostly in fragmentary flashbacks, is direct. In some cases, however, it is lyrical, as when Morrison tells of the neighbors' disaffection from Baby Suggs and Sethe, or Denver's fear of her mother and devotion to Beloved. The subtlety and ambiguity of the language sometimes does not stand up to the harsh facts that shape those feelings. When Sethe expresses shame for fondly remembering the sycamores of Sweet Home and not the men who were lynched from them, Morrison successfully encapsulates the complexity of our relationship to slavery in a short, poetic paragraph. But to understand the bruised bond between Denver and Sethe and Denver and Beloved, we need more than the single chapter narrated by Denver late in the book, which gives only a slight indication of the fear and loneliness she has lived with all of her life.

Beloved is my sister. I swallowed her blood right along with my mother's milk. The first thing I heard after not hearing anything was the sound of her crawling up the stairs. She was my secret company until Paul D. came. And I do. Love her. I do. She played with me and always came to be with me whenever I needed her. She's mine, Beloved. She's mine.

This passage is a striking parallel to Beloved's surreal explication of her obsession with Sethe; however, a stronger grounding in what life was like for Denver, Sethe, and Baby Suggs before the slaveowner arrived to take them back might have tied the characters together more tightly. This is not to say that *Beloved* is in any way a disappointment, except in that we want more of it. Sethe refers often to her "rememory" of the past, and it is this that

I needed. For it is surely in the "rememory" of the past that we recognize the people we have become.

When the ghost of the baby girl is finally banished and the neighbors readmit Sethe and Denver to their circle, they do what they can to forget Beloved. "This is not a story to pass on," they say. But, of course this is one of the many stories that must be passed on, particularly to the Africans who became the Negroes who are becoming the Afro-Americans of today. To lose these stories and their details is simply another aspect of slavery.

Morrison's style embraces the solid mysticism of African thought, creating a palpable aura like the scent she describes: "The closer the roses got to death, the louder their scent, and everybody who attended the carnival associated it with the stench of rotten roses. It made them a little dizzy and very thirsty but did nothing to extinguish the eagerness of the colored people filing down the road." Morrison evokes this history and the sensations with a power and poignancy untapped by any other prose writer working today.

JEWELLE GOMEZ is the author of eight books, including the cult favorite novel *The Gilda Stories* (soon to have a sequel). A previous version of this review appeared in *Belles Lettres: A Review of Books by Women* [04-88; V.3; N.4, p.4].

CHAPTER 3: *Jazz*

The Nobel laureate concludes her trilogy of interviews with Professor Emerita Angels Carabi by musing on the historical and musical background of Jazz, her most recent novel at the time.

As a general introduction to the book, I would first like to talk about the period of the 1920s, the postwar years after Reconstruction, when Black people moved from rural to urban places. What did this mean from the Black perspective? During Reconstruction, which occurred after 1865, two things happened. First, there was a lot of migration of Black people. They built towns, and in some places (particularly the West) they were very well organized and prosperous. There were over 100 Black towns in Oklahoma, with their own banks, schools, and churches — beautiful buildings. But there was also a huge backlash during Reconstruction. Blacks were attacked by white people, including the business community, because they were making a lot of money, were self-sufficient, and were on land that other people wanted. Then the lynchings began to increase. So there was a combination of dashed hopes of freedom after the war and some successes, because of the Black people in the Senate, the government, and so forth. Of course the huge repression of Black people prompted many of them to move to places like New York, Chicago, and Detroit — the big industrial centers, where there was safety in numbers and where they could make a good life.

World War I (like all the others) called Black men to serve. So many young Black men had gone to Europe and India, in all-Black battalions, and they suffered the way all soldiers did. They fought for the country that lynched them, and when they came back and wore their uniforms in many parts of the country, they were again lynched. There were a lot of emasculations ... surgical ones. People were snatched out of houses and burned, killed, or maimed. So the violence was particularly nasty after the war.

Somebody told me that in Tulsa (which had a well-protected, prosperous Black community), a Black boy was arrested on the alleged charge of rape. He was an elevator operator, and a white woman claimed he had made an indecent gesture toward her.

Nothing had actually happened — this is even what she said — and
he was innocent. So the Black people rescued him from prison
and took him into the Black neighborhood. When the authorities
came to get him, the people were armed, so the police blew up the
whole neighborhood with bombs. It wasn't just poverty that drove
Black people to the big cities. It was also success, because their
success was a major threat to the white population.

But the music also began to change in the 1920s. It always
changes, but this was the period of the seeds of jazz — instead of
the spiritual begging for relief or the coded language of escape
from slavery. Now you had musicians who played in bars, in
bordellos, or for entertainment. They began to express anger and
yearning, but they were confident ... and very seductive. So where
were the areas where you could claim freedom? You got into a big
city. There was the thrill of seeing yourself in large numbers, again
developing a sort of Black town: Harlem. There was a very
successful Black middle class in Brooklyn, but for everyday
people, one of the most interesting things was a freedom to fall in
love, to own your body, to be "immoral."

As far as Black people were concerned, white people always
put the stamp of immorality on them, even when the women were
forced to have babies. The accusation was not on the people who
forced them, but on the women who were forced — you know, as
usual. Anyway, some of the elements of that period seem so
pervasive because I think it affected America and the world. Jazz
became the sign of modernity, of a license that Black people
would try desperately to express.

In the little short life they had, that was how they felt good
about themselves, while fully aware of their difficulties. It was also
a postwar period, when there's always a lot of excitement, and
people wanted to finally be in the lead at this time of earthiness. It
was that spirit that was enabled by the music. I always see
background music to everything. In cultural terms, the period is
identified with white people, who symbolized it in literature.

The Great Gatsby, for instance?
Yes, F. Scott Fitzgerald is typical, and early Hemingway, John Dos
Passos, and Gertrude Stein. But the people who enabled the core

and the shape of that period were, of course, Black people, whose culture was evolving different things and being constantly invented and improvised. You had to stay alert to political changes, because you never knew what people were going to do at any moment. So you had to be always on guard and be able to adjust quickly. That ability was a double entendre: accommodating the grief we felt and the determination not to let life beat us up completely. The instinct for survival, plus "joie de vivre," was very important. The word *jazz* seems to encompass all of that, although its etymology has been contested. Most people agree that it is French "jism," meaning an ejaculation of semen. They used to call bordellos "jazz houses" because they were about sexual relations. And in these jazz houses, Black musicians played. So you can see that the word comes out of a vulgar, sexual term, which is why many Black musicians abhor it.

Black music's always called something — spiritual, gospel, jazz, boogie woogie, bop, bebop, rap — but it's never called music (for example, 20th-century music, modern music). So it's argued about in another way. White critics, in general, claim it as American. Which it is, but it's almost as though it was made with their culture, and so people have no part in it, except finally, to provide the music. To talk about it is to appropriate it. On one hand, art that is disseminated is good, that's what it was for. But on the other hand is the constant discrediting of the musicians and their impact: commercially, they made no money. The white people who imitated their music made money. The "King of Swing" was Benny Goodman! The jazz musicians went to Europe for recognition and appreciation of their music, because the Europeans in the '20s were aficionados and the white Americans were not, except in a sort of bland or played-down reproduction of it. So the music got a lot of security and satisfaction in Europe that it did not get in the States until very late. The white musicians were feeding off of it, claiming it as their own, but the original musicians were unable to get aesthetic and critical acclaim there.

I believe the 20s began to be the moment when Black culture, rather than American culture, began to alter the whole country, and eventually the western world. It was an overwhelming development in terms of excitement and glamour, and the sense of individualizing ourselves swept the world. So that's why I used the term *jazz*, because it sums all this up. But nobody in the book would call it that. In the States, it's always associated with something vulgar, which is part of its anarchy. It has implications of sex, violence, and chaos — all of which I wanted in the book.

Nobody agrees on anything about jazz (except that it survived beautifully and blossomed), but everybody thinks they know all about it, anywhere in the world. There is an interesting ownership of jazz. So, when I was thinking of who was going to tell this story, the idea of "who owns jazz," or who knows about it, came up. I was looking for a voice and having trouble figuring it out, but then I decided that the voice would be one of assumed knowledge, the voice that says, "I know everything." This is a kind of dominant ownership: without sex, gender, or age. Because the voice has to actually imagine the story it's telling using the art of imagination. It's in trouble, because if it's really involved in the process of telling the story and letting the other voices speak, the story that it thought it knew turns out to be entirely different from what it predicted because the characters will be evolving within the story, within the book.

It reminded me of a jazz performance in which the musicians are on stage. And they know what they are doing, they rehearse, but the performance is open to change, and the other musicians have to respond quickly to that change. Somebody takes off from a basic pattern, then the others have to accommodate themselves. That's the excitement, the razor's edge of a live performance of jazz. Now, in improvising on the spot in front of an audience, you find yourself in a place you could not possibly predict. But what happens when you go to this unpredictable place is that you are frequently taken into a room that you could not possibly have found if you had gone the normal way.

So, then the voice realizes, after hearing other voices, that the narrative is not going to be at all what it predicted. The more it learns about the characters (and they are not what the voice thought), it has to go on, but it goes on with more knowledge. The voice says, *"Now know. Now I know."* It began to imagine another kind of life taking place. You could never imagine those two could reconcile, but they are able to — not because the voice says so, but because the voice discovers who they are. I was trying to align myself with more interesting and intricate aspects of my notion of jazz as a demanding, improvisatory art form, so I had to get rid of the conventions, which I distrust. I've done this in other places, but not as radically as here. The thing is, I could not think of the voice of a person. I know everybody refers to "I" as a woman (because I'm a woman, I guess), but for me, it was very important that the "I" would say what a typical book would limit itself to, what a physical book would say. The book uses verbs — "I think," "I believe," "I wonder," "I imagine," "I know" — but it never sits down, it never walks, because it's a book. The voice is the voice of a talking book. So when the voice says, "I know what it's like to be left standing when someone promises," it talks to the reader. It sounds like a very erotic, sensual love song of a person who loves you. This is a love song of a book talking to the reader. *[Morrison then recited the following passage from the novel.]*

> "I envy them their public love. I myself have only
> known it in secret, shared it in secret and longed,
> aw longed to show it — to be able to say out loud
> what they have no need to say at all: That I have
> loved only you, surrendered my whole self, reckless
> to you and nobody else. That I want you to love me
> back and show it to me. That I love the way you
> hold me, how close you let me be to you. I like
> your fingers on and on, lifting, turning. I have
> watched your face for a long time now, and missed
> your eyes when you went away from me. Talking to
> you and hearing you answer — that's the kick. But I
> can't say that aloud; I can't tell anyone that I have
> been waiting for this all my life and that being
> chosen to wait is the reason I can. If I were able I'd
> say it. Say make me, remake me. You are free to
> do it and I am free to let you because look, look.
> Look where your hands are. Now."

It's a book talking, but few people read it like that. Most reviewers said "she [I mean Toni Morrison] is pleading with the reader to forgive her." It was interesting to me how the whole act of reading, holding, surrendering to a book, is part of that beautiful intimacy of reading. When it's tactile, your emotions are deeply involved; if it's a good book, if you're just there. I deliberately restricted myself by using an "I" that was only connected to the artifact of the book as an active participant in the invention of the story of the book, as though the book were talking, writing itself, in a sense. It's an interesting and overwhelming technical idea to me. But also it gave me an opportunity to check the actor, performance, style, without knowing the play, knowing what the next movement is going to be, and then getting caught up in it, and then having to invent something new, the more you get involved in it. It's very strange, but I like it because it's risky. But jazz unsettles you. You always feel a little on edge. "Did I catch it?" Then you have to listen again. You're not in control. It was this assumption of control, the reader's control, the book's control — all of these had to be displaced, so no one's in control.

Tell me about Dorcas. Initially, part of her story reminds me of Sula in the sense that she learns about the unexpectedness of death, and that keeps her silent.
She decides to throw herself into it.

Exactly. Because she has experienced that, then she is ready to go to the limit.
Dorcas is just straining at the bit the way her aunt has overprotected her. You can imagine the adoration that an older man can bring to a young girl, particularly at that age. It's so flattering and you're so empowered by it, and you can manipulate him for attention and that's terribly exciting. And then once she gets real strength from Joe, she gets an identity, she feels empowered. Then she goes to this other guy. She feels like a woman, but the source of her feeling like that has come from Joe. Oh! That stupidness, that sort of girlish, goopy feeling. But if you look at her from Felice's point of view, she was always interested in a kind of a wanton power. She would get guys to do things for her. She was always a little bit of — not an outcast — but a little bit different from the other girls.

Felice begins to doubt whether their friendship was really true friendship. And Felice learns a great deal from exploring the relationship and talking to Joe and Violet and rethinking what is going on. Even if there was that strong affection between them, she knew that Dorcas didn't like her enough to stay alive because she let herself die. Felice gets to think back, let herself think about how she was with men and decide not to be like that. She's the one who was to go out and face the world and become somebody who was independent of all that.

But yet she can put herself in perspective of that relationship, so in the end even the voice says, Felice is nobody's ham and she's nobody's toy. And she's walking to a new tune, she's like the future — as Denver [in *Beloved*] is the future. She says "I want to be independent. I want to work. I don't want to be a prostitute." And she's looking like that experience has been good for her [and] sad for her.... She has learned a lot from it, I think. And she's more likely to be a coherent personality. She will never be somebody else's side chick again.

And she brings the records and the music and then Joe dances.
That's right. She brings music to the awful house and they dance. So jazz enables possibility once again. Because it's when, narratively speaking, Joe feels better. He knows that he's sort of killed Dorcas but she helped kill herself, so that lightens his load a little bit.

Wild puzzles me a lot.
Wild is a kind of Beloved. The dates are the same. You see a pregnant Black woman naked at the end of *Beloved.* It's at the same time, you know back in the Golden Gray section of *Jazz*, [that] there is a crazy woman out in the woods. The woman they call Wild (because she's sort of out of it from the hit on the head) could be Sethe's daughter, Beloved. When you see Beloved towards the end, you don't know; she's either a ghost who has been exorcised or she's a real person pregnant by Paul D, who runs away ending up in Virginia, which is right next to Ohio. But I don't want to make all these connections.

Remember I was talking about those Black towns? Most of them disappeared, but I'm going to project one that moved away from the collapse of an original Black town and set up in Oklahoma. They went from being very rebellious, to being progressive, to stability. Then they got compromised and reactionary and were unable to adjust to new things happening. The novel is called *Paradise.*

JAZZ: Passionate Riffs
A review by Faye Moskowitz (1992)

Toni Morrison's sixth novel, like much of her other work, is an exploration of the manifestations and consequences of unrefined passion. In Morrison's previous novel, *Beloved,* the hideous institution of slavery stands not as the focus but rather the backdrop for Sethe's unspeakable act of infanticide. Sethe kills her baby because of a love so strong she would rather have her dead than consigned to a life as a slave. The kaleidoscopic turns of the plot form and reform themselves to illuminate both the reasons for her crime and her ultimate expiation and redemption. *Jazz,* too, is about passion. In the book's first paragraph, we learn that a door-to-door salesman of beauty products, Joe Trace, "fell for an eighteen-year-old with one of those deep down spooky loves that made him so sad and happy he shot her just to keep the feeling going." Joe's wife, Violet (sometimes known to the community as "Violent") goes to the funeral parlor in a jealous rage intending to slash the dead girl's face with a knife.

As with *Beloved,* you need to stand back from this book, get some distance, circle it the way you might a painting that pulses so with color and design that the first glance bewilders, maybe even puts you off. Yet, inevitably, the art form you think of is jazz. The story of Joe, Violet, and the girl Dorcas provides a kind of recurring melody, while chapter after chapter goes off on improvisational riffs, changing point of view, moving backward and forward in time, always echoing, embellishing, and deepening the original theme.

Joe and Violet first meet cutting cane in Virginia. They come north to New York in the "Colored Section of the Southern Sky," and here the true passion of the novel begins, for the City has rarely been pictured so sensuously and optimistically. Morrison evokes New York, particularly Harlem as it appeared to blacks in the 1920s: "Here comes the new Look out. There goes the sad stuff. The bad stuff. The way everybody was then and there. Forget that. History is over, you all, and everything's ahead at last." As in *Beloved,* where the ghost of a dead baby haunts Sethe's house, so the ghost of a baby that never was can be felt fleetingly throughout

Jazz. The young Joe and Violet, self-sufficient in their love, do not mourn the babies they lose to miscarriages. Only later does Violet long for a child, when she is too old to conceive, and Joe seeks solace in a girl young enough to be his daughter. Like the power of negative space, absence takes on an importance of its own. As Joe mourns Dorcas, "He minds her death, is so sorry about it, but minded more the possibility of his memory failing to conjure up the dearness."

But Violet mourns too. She mourns the loss of her husband's passion and drinks endless malteds, hoping to gain back her once powerful hips. Eaten with envy, she imagines Joe and Dorcas sitting together at the Indigo nightclub, while Dorcas's hand, "the one that wasn't holding the glass shaped like a flower, was under the table drumming out a rhythm on the inside of his thigh, his thigh, his thigh, thigh, thigh...." When Violet insinuates herself into the home of Alice Manfred, the aunt who raised Dorcas, hoping to learn more about the girl who bewitched her husband, the two women unaccountably become friends.

Like Baby Suggs in *Beloved,* Alice is wise woman, one of the elders Morrison so admires. Standing at the ironing board, turning a wrinkled blouse into a work of art with starch and steam at her iron, she listens as Violet says, "We born around the same time, me and you.... We women, me and you. Tell me something real. Don't just say I'm grown and ought to know. I don't. I'm fifty and I don't know nothing. What about it? Do I stay with him? I want to. I think. I want ... well, I didn't always ... now I want some fat in this life." And Alice gives her essentially the same message Baby Suggs gives Sethe. Alice says, "Wake up. Fat or lean, you just got one. This is it." But she is quick to point out she isn't talking about passivity. "Nobody's asking you to take it," she says. "I'm saying make it, make it!"

Sections in *Jazz* will take your breath away. They sing like a Lester Young solo, but in the end the melody line eludes you. The mysterious, omniscient voice confuses rather than enlightens. Still, this is carping. Morrison at her best is glorious. Even at her less than best, she is the envy of most other fiction writers.

FAYE MOSKOWITZ is the author of *A Leak in the Heart, And the Bridge Is Love: Life Stories, Whoever Finds This I Love You,* and *Peace in the House: Tales from a Yiddish Kitchen.* A previous version of this review appeared in *Belles Lettres: A Review of Books by Women* [Summer 1992; V.7, N.4, p.4]

AFTERWORD

"Whenever Belles Lettres *arrives in the mail, it's like greeting a trusted, thoughtful, and well-travelled friend who is going to tell me the books I most want and need to read. Its reviews connect women's writings to their traditions, criticize in a way that helps writers make our work better, and always remember that women's ideas must stand the test of women's experience."*

These sentiments from longtime reader Gloria Steinem captured perfectly the founding editors' intentions for *Belles Lettres: A Review of Books by Women,* which premiered in 1984 as a forum for celebrating, promoting, and preserving literature by women. The editorial mix included timely reviews; original poetry, photographs, and personal essays; interviews, rediscoveries, and retrospectives; and theme sections based on ethnic, national, and cultural groupings. We considered titles from both trade and independent presses, with an emphasis on supporting the work of noncommercial literary ones.

From the outset, *Belles Lettres* cultivated diversity through the books chosen and the reviewers who engaged with them. We spotlighted Jewish, African American, Latina, and Asian authors, and we covered the international scene through special sections on writing from Australia, the former Soviet Union, Eastern Europe, Africa, Latin America and more.

Belles Lettres was accessible to and enjoyed by the general reader, as well as being valued by librarians and academics. We were quoted frequently in *Contemporary Literary Criticism* and in *Black Literature Criticism.* Our readers appreciated the attention to international writing, the works by women of color, and the interviews and rediscoveries. Our reviews and essays focused on literary writing, and we sought to assign pieces to creative writers and informed educators/scholars.

Our first bimonthly issue, in September 1985, was a 16-page tabloid. Our final one was a 100-page, tri-quarterly magazine with a glossy cover. As well as prizing good content, we strove for excellence in design and typography. The Spring 1994 issue debuted a contemporary redesign, and Spring 1995 was laid out

with the snazziest desktop publishing technology at the time —
WordPerfect!

In January 1992, *Belles Lettres* was one of nine nonprofit
literary magazines to be awarded an audience development grant
from the Lila Wallace–Reader's Digest Literary Magazine
Marketing Development Program. In Phase I (1991–92), we
created a marketing and organizational development plan, which
led to our being funded with the requested amount. In Phase II
(1993–94), we tested several large-scale marketing approaches.
Although we lacked the cash to capitalize on our direct mail test
data, we doubled our paid circulation in the two years of the grant.
We also paid our authors for the first time ... hallelujah! (Unlike
many other literary magazines, we had no institutional sponsor. All
of the editors volunteered their time, effort, and expertise.)

Then the boom fell. It was known from the start that two of the
magazines would be dropped from the grant's final phase, and
Belles Lettres became one of them. Next our distributor folded,
owing us a substantial sum. These events left us with a completed
issue and insufficient capital for printing and mailing it. Although
we had been gathering momentum for a major breakthrough in
circulation and advertising income, we lost our mojo, so to speak,
and no amount of striving could get it back.

Yet in our 10 years of publishing we succeeded in spotlighting
myriad facets of women's writing, from "Nu Shu" (an ancient
script and art of poetry practiced by rural Chinese women), to an
elegy for a book collection lost in Hurricane Hugo, an essay by
novelist Carole Maso on the state of commercial publishing to a
section on women of the American West, to the groundbreaking
work of the inimitable Lynda Barry (currently a MacArthur
Foundation grantee). We were particularly proud of our
interviews; for example, we published a rare, illuminating one with
Toni Morrison in 1988, and after the publication of *Beloved* and
Jazz, the wondrous scholar Angels Carabi followed up with two
more installments. Ms. Carabi, one of our contributing editors, was
awarded a grant from the Spanish government to speak with 13
women writers of color living in the US; *Belles Lettres* helped
coordinate her itinerary and published many of the conversations.

We also collaborated with the University of Michigan Press on a collection of our interviews with female poets. *Truthtellers of the Times,* featured Robin Becker, Gwendolyn Brooks, Lucille Clifton, Lucha Corpi, Rita Dove, Joy Harjo, Josephine Jacobsen, June Jordan, Janice Mirikitani, Alicia Ostriker, Linda Pastan, Minnie Bruce Pratt, May Miller Sullivan, and Karen Swenson, with an introduction by Toi Derricote. And in tandem with the National Museum of Women in the Arts, we developed a reading series with emerging, established, and legendary authors (e.g., Jacqueline Woodson, Faye Moskowitz, Linda Hogan, Sandra Cisneros, Elena Poniatowska, Faye Myenne Ng, Edwidge Danticat, Maryse Conde, and Tillie Olsen). Another highlight was bringing the incomparable short story writer Grace Paley to the museum to coach aspiring young authors from the Washington, DC area.

In Fall 1994, the Women's National Book Association presented me, as founding editor/publisher, with the "Bookwoman of the Year" award, citing an "enduring and unique contribution to the world of books, and through books, to society." (Past recipients included Blanche Knopf, Eleanor Roosevelt, Pearl Buck, Lillian Smith, and Rachel Carson.) I shared this honor with all of the women who gave their time and expertise unstintingly so that the review could flourish. In accepting it, I emphasized the outpouring of reprints, anthologies, translations, and original publications bringing literature by women to the general reader.

Throughout our history, the women of *Belles Lettres* have been honored to do our part in furthering an awareness of what Gloria Naylor once called "the feast awaiting women and men in need of a balanced perspective on the richness existing in American and world literature." The banquet endures, so please take a seat at the table and dig in! *—Janet Palmer Mullaney*

UPDATES ON THE CONTRIBUTORS

ANGELS CARABI is a Professor Emerita of English literature at the University of Barcelona. Her special interest is women writers of color from the U.S., a great many of whom she has interviewed.

JEWELLE GOMEZ's trilogy of plays about African American artists in the first half of the 20th century (*Waiting for Giovanni, Leaving the Blues, Unpacking in Ptown*; available on Amazon) was commissioned and produced by New Conservatory Theatre Center in San Francisco and The Other Side of Silence (TOSOS) Company in New York.

FAYE MOSKOWITZ is a Professor Emerita of English literature at George Washington University. Her interests are creative writing (particularly the memoir and the short story), as well as Jewish-American literature from 1645 to the present. Her books include *A Leak in the Heart: Tales from a Woman's Life* (1985), *Whoever Finds This: I Love You* (1988), *And the Bridge Is Love: Life Stories* (1991), and *Peace in the House: Tales from a Yiddish Kitchen* (2002).

We owe an enormous debt of gratitude to the reviewers, copy- and consulting editors, donors, subscribers, and other enthusiasts of women's literature who contributed to our publishing history in myriad ways. Brava! This collection is dedicated to you.

Special kudos go to longtime supporters Dawna Jonte (an ally par excellence) and Karen Tucker Jenkins (who managed our subscriptions, gratis). Karen also appeared of late as a guardian angel to offer financial support while I prepared this initial volume in a series that interested parties have envisioned for decades. If all goes well, it will be followed by several more thematic collections on women writers you may know and love, as well as many others — perhaps some discovered for the first time.

—*JPM*